Inspired

Nicola

An unconventional collection of poetry

First Edition

Copyright © Nicola Dady 2015

Edited by Joanne Li & David Weale- Cochrane

Printed and bound By Amazon Create Space

All rights reserved. No part of this book may be reproduced, transmitted, or stored in a retrieval system or by any form without the prior permission of the author.

For Jermayne

I have a gift, 'The Gift of Words'. I am able to translate life, as I see it into beautiful, yet thought provoking and brutally honest arrangements which many readers may be able to relate to.

I have travelled many roads, some real smooth and safe, others broken and dangerous. But always persevere.

Life has taught me to appreciate everything and everyone in my world and that real, unconditional love and happiness comes from within.

Be inspired. Be happy. Spread love.

Acknowledgements.

Firstly I would like to thank god, for trusting me with this precious gift of mine. I am so thankful that I am able to inspire and encourage others with my words.

I would like to give a special thanks to Jermayne. You believed in me and helped me to acquire the confidence to be able to share my words with the world. You saw the potential in me when I was blind to it. You also inspired many of my pieces. I will forever be grateful. Love always x

Shenai and Corey, you inspire me to be a better person. You light up my life and I am so proud to call you my children. I love you x

My Girls… Kim, Seana, Colleen, Donna, Kelly, Louise, Stacey, Juanita, Lisa J, Sam, Mishal, Mel, Celina, Maydha, Gail, Vicki, Lynn and Maggie. Thank you so much for believing in me and being there to support me and for all the jokes and laughter we have shared. I love you.

My Boys…. Ross, Matthew, Justin, Jason, Mikey, Lloyd, Teddy, Jamie, Duane, David and Adjekum. Big, Big, Big Love for looking out for me, for guiding, protecting, advising and supporting me. I appreciate you all.

Mum, Granny, Mum Georgina, Aunty Avril, Aunty Ivy, Josette and Julie. My mother figures. For the nurturing, knowledge and wisdom you have all shared with me. You have shaped me into the woman I am today. Thank you for raising me.

Joanne and David Thank you so much for proof-reading and editing this book. I appreciate the support. Big love to you both.

Tim Welburn Thanks for finding the time to format my book. Without you I would have been lost. I appreciate you,

Lastly I would like to thank each and every one of you who have bought this book. You are making my dreams come true. I really hope you enjoy it and are inspired. Peace and love to you all x

Contents

Take advice from the flowers and bloom

Nature's Way
A Simple Leaf
Floating
From Sunshine to Rainy Days
I Fly
No Fear
Rain
The Robin
The Moon
Set Me Free
Home

Love is all

A True Friend
Bonnie and Clyde
Consumed with love
Inspired By Love
Love
Soulmate
Spread Love
Proud
Dear Son
How Can Love Just Disappear?
Where are you?
Why
Chemo
My Special stuff
Dear Friend

Open Your Eyes

Mixed
Gold Digger
Mirrors
August Riots
Nothing Ever Stays The Same
Baby Mother
R.I.P Mark Duggan
Free Your Minds
Who's Sick
Consumer Consumption

The Dark Side

If I Go To Sleep
Grim Reaper
Flashbacks
Cancer Filled Room
Haiku
Tears
Silence

I See The Light

It's Not That Bad
Soldier
You Will Get By

If You Don't laugh, You Cry

The Last Lamb Chop
I Ain't Giving Up My Seat
I Can't Stand Spoiled Kids
Beware Of The Feeder

"Take advice from the flowers and bloom."

Nature's Way

A little seed was planted now we sit back and watch it grow

With the freeness of the wild grass which carpets a meadow

Like long blades intertwining and dancing gently in the breeze

To the music they make - moving, quiet soulful melodies.

Like all things unexpected this has come as a surprise

And it's hard to piece together what's been right before our eyes.

So now we've let it out,

No more secrets no more lies,

Let's let our lights shine together and make our own sunrise.

A Simple Leaf

Most people don't see the beauty of a simple leaf.

I do, I notice every crease.

From the veins that feed the smooth blade,

To the original print uniquely placed.

From the base to the apex I soak in the wonder,

I inspect it thoroughly caress the rough surface under.

The vibrant colour in the adolescent phase,

The change of appearance that comes with age.,

I cherish this blade all the same.

From a million leaves I chose this one.

For it comes from the same stem which I am from.

I know every scar, from battering winds

And tiny cuts which pierce the skin.

I know and love each and every one.

Love which magnifies ever long.

Visions of handsomeness imprinted in my mind

Of the delicate leaf which I stay close by.

Most people don't notice the beauty of a simple leaf.

I do... I notice every crease.

Floating

I am lighter than a single feather floating in the breeze,

                                          I go where ever I want,

                    I do whatever I please,

I follow no instruction

And break all the rules,

                        Take no advice from brainwashed fools,

I float on water, I glide up high.

                            There are no limits up here in the sky.

I move so elegantly full of grace

                        As I know I'm the winner of my own race.

Oh how exciting it is to move blindly, not worried about where life may find me.

When the wind settles and my journey is complete,

there will be an abundance of happiness and love with no sign of defeat!

From Sunshine to Rainy Days

Oh how good the sun felt when it beamed upon my skin,
Such a happy, warm content feeling that I felt from deep within.
The smiles were uncontrollable,
My cheeks stuck in a grin
And that little voice inside was saying

WIN

WIN

WIN

Just as sudden as the sun came out the grey clouds clambered in
And I could feel the little goose pimples raising in my skin.
There was a storm coming,
I recognised the smell
But instead of running for cover, I prayed the bad weather would dispel.

Just like the rain,
My tears dropped.
I hoped the storm would go away,
Wished I could turn back the clock.
I wait for the blue sky to reappear,
So this horrible feeling inside will disappear.
When the birds sing again
And the atmosphere clears
And the smile beams on my face from ear to ear.

I Fly

I have my wings

So I can fly

I'm flying so high

You can't reach me

I'm flying so fast

You can't catch me

I glide so gracefully

You can't see my movements

I am free

Free as a bird in flight

I fly forward

NEVER looking back.

Please don't watch and envy

Though it's not easy to do

Just listen and believe what your heart says

And you will take flight too.

No Fear

A gentle breeze

    A sandy shore

        The more I opened up

    The more I saw

    The less I looked

The more I stared

    I focused so deep

        I wasn't scared

    Something happened

Right then and there.

    I inhaled LIFE and exhaled FEAR!!

Rain

I'm lying in my bed and I'm listening to the rain,

And I can't help but think about snuggling with Jermayne.

The comfort I feel when he is here

Matches the raindrops melody in my ear.

When his arms wrap around me and he strokes my hair

There is no better place to be I swear.

The Robin

There once was a Robin red breast,
Who would sit upon my fence.
I would stare at him for hours,
Wondering how long he would rest?

He would stop by my garden,
Each and every day.
He would perch and discern,
Then he would swiftly fly away.

I would await him every morning,
Listening out for his cheerful chirp.
Along he would come as predicted,
Downing feathers and looking alert.

He would take in the environment,
So relaxed and on his own
I would often sit and speculate,
Did he have a family? A home?

The red and fluffy feathers
They orbited his chest.
He would groom them until immaculate
So he looked his very best.

One day I sat and waited
For my little friend to arrive.
He didn't then or ever again,
This took me by surprise.

I often wonder what happened
To my handsome Robin mate.
Did he find a family?
Did he succumb to fate?

I miss that Robin Red Breast
That I came to know.
I look for him from time to time.
Why did he have to go?

The Moon

When I look up at your face
I smile
So glad you came
If only for a while.

You just linger and listen
No comment in sight
But I know you are there
So that makes it alright

Sometimes when I see you
You are brighter than normal
You look so strong
Seem so formal

Your brightness
It fills my dark
I feel your comfort
You warm my heart

Your handsome stature
Always composed
Amazingly beautiful
Your power glows

Right through my window
It fills the room
I sleep so peacefully
Being guided by the moon

Set Me Free

The little bird who is trapped in a cage,

Fills with emotion which fuels her rage.

Being teased with the vision of beautiful sights

Whilst kept captive, trapped day and night.

Always standing to attention, jumping at every sound.

Wondering how it feels to be free and proud.

Thinking of adventures yet to be had.

Conducting escape routes in her head.

Biting the bars with a worn down beak,

Wishing someone could understand what she speaks.

The people on the outside looking in

Are in awe of her beauty and the way she sings.

They smile and compliment her beautiful song

Not noticing something is dreadfully wrong.

Her songs are filled with sadness and despair,

She begs "Please unclip my wings and let me out of here."

But with the beauty of her cry,

They enjoy her songs

Whilst they briefly stop, then move along.

So she cries her song as she dreams of beyond....

Let me be

Set me free

Set me free

Home

I sift through memories and dreams

Searching for something I know that I've seen

Completely unsure of what I will find

But not at all scared to leave what I know behind

Absolutely unsettled, awake or asleep

Until I hear the sound of your heartbeat

Head pressed on your chest I am able to rest

And I realise

I am Home

So I've moved around, lived in a few towns

Undecided and never content

In my heart there's a place that I've seemed to misplace

But I don't know if I've even been there yet

Always rearranging and forever changing

Is what I seem to do best

Then your arms wrap around and I know I've been found

And I'm sure that

I am home.

"Love is all."

A True Friend

A friend should be caring, **loving** and giving

Not mean, hateful or unforgiving

A REAL friend is one who will be there for you

In good times AND bad times they encourage you through

An unconditional **love** which you both must share

A person you trust whether far or near

Someone you can laugh with

Someone you don't fear

Someone who doesn't just talk

But who also can hear

A true friend is so hard to find

So when you do gain one, be sure to be kind

Be honest and considerate and never cross the line

And your friendship will stand the test of time.

Bonnie and Clyde

Let me share your pain

Let me have half, I'll take the strain

Let me hear all that's on your mind

Let me listen intently as you unwind

Let me stroke your skin

Let me watch you heal from within.

Let me kiss your tear stained cheeks

Let me caress your tired feet

Let me rock you in my arms

Let me rub both of your palms

Let me softly sing you to sleep

Let me be the shoulder on which you weep.

Let me be the one who makes you smile.

Let me be the one who makes it all worthwhile.

Let me be the Bonnie to your Clyde

Babe let me ride or die...

Consumed With Love

In this moment I am completely and utterly consumed with

LOVE.

It comes through the phone via calls and texts,

It comes from the little fingers which hug my neck,

It comes from the man who plants kisses on my lips,

It comes from his skin under my fingertips,

It comes from the coolness of the midnight breeze,

It comes from the shedding of the blossoming trees,

It comes from the embrace of the almighty!

Love finds its way and smothers me........

And this I am truly thankful for.

Inspired By Love

Don't feel sad or cry today

Instead smile because you'll laugh again someday!

Don't cry because of pain you feel instead be thankful you're breathing still.

Don't dwell on bad feelings you may hide inside

Just learn from the happiness of an innocent child

When your day goes from bad to worse,

Give a homeless person the change from your purse.

Give and you will get in return a beautiful feeling no work can earn.

Appreciate all the positive things

And all the blessings that life will bring.

Allow yourself to understand that highs and lows are never planned

But **love** changes everything

It brings a warm feeling from deep within.

Don't be scared to open your heart,

And even if not fully make a small start.

Love the way your eyes have sight,

And that you hear every sound at night.

Love the lips you have to speak,

For you are able to talk and say your piece.

Love the way your able to stand,

And are free to explore this wondrous land.

Love the birds, the trees, the breeze,

The tiny ants and the minute fleas, as they are blessed with life just as we.

Love that you have family and close friends.

Be **thankful** for each one is God sent.

Appreciate the little things, focus on all that **happiness** that **love** will bring.

Love the mirror that hangs on the wall.

Love the reflection looking back at you most of all!

Love

If you take my heart

Please handle it with care

For its delicate and fragile

That's why I never share

I keep it locked within

Behind barriers and bars

If you manage to break it out

Please don't deface it with scars

Just **love** me

That's all I want

Just **love** me

Soulmate

I can feel your emotion

I can see your soul

I can touch your spirit

As the force evolves.

You can heal my sickness

You can lift my heart

You can talk to me without speaking

Even when we are apart.

Subconsciously connected

Our minds are intertwined

Our souls they dance together

Our hearts eternally bind

Spread Love

I will not judge

I will not hate

I will not sit down and speculate.

I will not gossip

I will not take sides

I will not try work out or wonder why

I will not be angry

I will not be scared

I will not read or listen to views impaired.

I WILL spread LOVE though.

Proud

Beauty beyond belief,

The wide smile with those perfect teeth.

Eyes which light up the sky.

Hair curly, brown and wild.

So very funny at times,

Confident with a hint of shy.

Not an ounce of bad inside,

Always helping, giving and kind.

At times I watch you, when you can't see,

I'm amazed how much you are like me.

And I am proud, as proud can be

Of my amazing, beautiful, grown up baby!!

Dear Son

I want to tell you a secret, one to help you on your way, you may not need it now but it will mean something one day.

It's a secret about women, and how to treat the right one well, so you can keep her happy and in turn you happy as well.

If you are blessed enough to find it, **love** is a beautiful thing. If she cares and loves you genuinely, son give that girl a ring!!

Notice everything she does for you, especially things that are free, if she cooks, cleans, looks out for you son, get down on your knee.

Appreciate ALL of the small stuff like having a clean pair of socks, having your shirts ironed and comfort when you're feeling rough.

Listen when she says she **loves** you, for she is giving you her heart, cherish those words dearly and you will surely never part.

Other women will try and seduce you and you might just get the urge. But just remember before you cheat, this treatment **love** don't deserve.

Don't sleep around casually whilst in a **loving** home, don't hurt her with your antics and lead her eye to roam.

Please, son, be a man of your word and keep her your only one. Treat her as a queen, or better still like your mum..

You see a woman who **loves** will move mountains to support her man, so respect this wonderful woman, and treat her like no other man can.

Give yourself to her fully, and trust her with your heart, make a strong foundation, marriage is a good place to start.

Stop thinking that there might be, someone better out here, unless you are prepared to give up all you have right there.

Scoop her up and **love** her, protect her from any harm, show her that she is important, show her off as your lucky charm.

Shower her with compliments, boast about her to your friends, and make her feel secure as not just your woman but your friend.

Never ever hit her, no matter how angry you get, as you can never turn back time and you'll be filled with guilt and regret.

Son I know this is a lot of advice that I'm passing on to you, but I believe that it's important I share this stuff with you.

You can trust me son, for I will never lie to you, I only want you to do the best in everything you do.

Love mum x

How Can Love Just Disappear

How can love just disappear?

I was 99% certain it was here.

Along with the mixed up emotions of happiness and fear.

I could have sworn it touched my heart,

I felt it here.

Makes me really wonder if it was truly there??

If it was,

Then how could love just disappear?

Where are you?

It's 3.am
Where are you?
I can't sleep
Don't know what to do
I'm alone
Waiting for you
Wondering what you're up to

                                                     It's 3:20
                                      Time has passed
                 Time from love that's meant to last
                                I call your phone
                                        No answer
                              Are you ok I wonder?
                         I can't take the silence

It's 4am
I realise
You're not coming back tonight
You made a choice
To let me sleep alone
You made a choice to not come home
You made a choice to not answer your phone.

                                                 It's 4:30
                                 The birds are awake
                                      And so am I
                 I guess I'll loose a nights sleep
           And you will reach your sexual peak
                                  I'm happy for you
                             And sad for myself

It is what it is.

Why

I say I love myself but I know this isn't true.

Because if I did, why would I hurt myself the way I do?

Why is it ok for me to love without it in return?

Why do I make the same mistakes, will I never learn?

Why do I do things that I know will only end in tears?

Why can't I show emotion or let go of burden and fears?

Why do I apologise for what I believe to be right?

Why do I promise people things when the best they can give me is 'might' ?

Why do I hide my feelings just to protect those of others?

Why do I keep secrets and worry they might be discovered?

When will I find true love and passion for myself?

When will I stop acting tough and just accept some help!

Chemo

As the virus takes hold of my body
My muscles aching with pain
The hot and cold flushes
A shock as it shoots through my veins
A regular procedure, in an oh so familiar place
It's such an unpleasant feeling
But something inevitably I must face.
Although the surrounding is comfortable
It saddens me to realise
The reason behind this routine
As I do the tears fill my eyes.
The emotion is overwhelming
The courage is fading inside
All I've secretly yearned for is someone to comfort me
And bring the smile out from inside.
I've battled through this on many occasion,
Every stage being carefully planned
But this time it's much easier to cope with
Because he is holding my hand.

My Special Stuff

My candy floss, my daydream

My light of day, my sun screen.

The pillow I hold close at night

The seatbelt on a late night flight.

The warmth from an open flame

The hood that shields me from the rain

The pain killer which numbs the pain

That feeling when I've won a game.

The massive smile upon my face

The comfort of a warm embrace.

The senses on my naked skin

when covered by black,

smooth satin.

The butterfly flutter deep inside

The happy tears of a newlywed bride

The way a mother is filled with pride

The excitement felt on a fast ride.

How complete I feel when by your side.

Love....

Dear Friend

I'm writing this with a warmness inside
With the space in my heart that you reside.
Never have I felt this feeling before
For a friend of mine so I cannot ignore.
I want you to know just how much you mean to me
Like the wind of the air and the waves in the sea.
Like the stars in the universe on a clear sky's night
Like the strength not to lay down but to get up to fight.
You Inspire me daily with your beautiful mind
With the love you share and the peace that we find.
With the jokes that we share with no judgement at all
With our daily phone calls on the way to school.
You are a special spirit and I'm proud of my girl
When you still love and laugh though your going through hell.
I love the sound of your voice and the realness of your cry
for as long as I live I'll be by your side.

I swear!

"Open Your Eyes"

Mixed

Is it really any wonder why my mind is confused..
One minute the abuser next minute the abused.

See if we look back into history, go way back in the day. One half of me is the captor the other half's the slave.

You see I am of mixed heritage, a black egg mixed with white sperm.
A pale brown experiment, oh boy there was a lot to learn!

Now when we go back in history, say 3000 years, my black bloodline was bought, traded, beaten and enslaved.
My white ancestors, however, were thought superior to the world, because their skin was white entitled power that bore racist boys and girls.

Is it any wonder I battle with wrongs and rights? In my mind there are two sides which constantly seem to fight..

You see my white ancestral family believed what was wrong was right. They had no intent of uniting, loving black people was not all right.

Raping my black sisters and keeping them as slaves, purchasing my black brothers using them as tools of trade.

My African descent, however, displayed much strength and fought and fought for freedom whilst held by shackles and restraints.

So why do people think I have the best of both worlds? Just because my skin is light and I have loose curls. I'm deemed terribly lucky because I carry black shape, my skin always looks tanned and my nose is straight!

But all of those qualities are superficial, all of these things DON'T make me special.

You see this is mixed blood that runs through my veins, all round my body and up into my brain. ..Which is fighting its own battle, trying to unite, sometimes unable to determine what's wrong from right. Other times I must say, positively strong. I just wish both parts would integrate and get on.

So yes I have the best of both of inner qualities from my past. But at times the worst too, leading me down the wrong paths...

Peace love and harmony is what I desire along with strength and perseverance to guide my god given power!

Gold Digger

I will be the first to confess that gold digging is what I do best.

You see I dig deep into the shadiest of minds

Looking for riches all the time, sifting through dirt and dark places only to find expressionless faces

And brainwashed minds with empty spaces.

Being a slave for my own kind. Searching and searching unsure if I'll find.

Working with no pay to benefit others,

My voice silenced,

oppressed

encapsulated

undiscovered

Soil stained my fingers blood on their hands, sifting for jewels in an old steel pan.

I find pain in the form of depression, Items of trade become obsessions, dependents of alcohol,

tobacco, legal drugs. Addicts of self harm, no passion or love

So I dig for gold,

but not the kind that shines, but the kind that will open and enrich my mind,

Yes I dig for what I believe in, to uncover the roots, and for all my labour to bathe in the fruits.

I'm not sure they exist, but I'm told they do, so when I find one myself I'll believe it true.

I'm searching for a black diamond...

Mirrors

Can you look yourself in the mirror?
I mean look into your eyes?
Do you quickly look away, or do you pose and smize?
Can you see the sadness that is buried deep inside?
Do you focus on your nose, mouth, freckles ignore issues, hide?

Can you stare yourself out, without feeling doubt?
Do you love yourself from the inside out?
Do you avoid catching eyes with your own reflection
As they show you all the pain and deception.

When you are angry have you ever examined your face?
Have you looked at your features when you are in a bad place?
Or do you walk past the mirror and not give a damn,
Think the people around you can't see who you can?

They can't avoid it though.

They see what you can't.

A miserable face, a thousand mistakes written all over it,
And they are very carefully placed.
You see the eyes are windows to your soul,
The unseen story, the never told,
The shame, the pain, the hurt the blame,
The tears you refuse to let out again.

Go on do it.
Face yourself,
Look right in the mirror and embrace yourself,
Keep connection and don't let go,
Heal the trauma that lives in your soul.

When the tears are ready let them spill,
Empty your feelings begin the process to heal.
Focus on the beauty that you can see.
Love yourself unconditionally.

You are only human, it's ok to make mistakes
We all suffer with pain and deep heartache.
Just lift the corners of your mouth from ear to ear
And watch the tears miraculously disappear.
Forgive yourself and accept yourself too
As that inner happiness lays within you.

Don't waste any time, get to it today.
Go look at yourself in a positive way.

August Riots

I watch the news astounded

Fused tightly my butt to the chair

I just cannot believe the madness

Can't ignore or refuse to care

It's so gut wrenching to witness

All I seem to do is cry

I see hundreds of angry faces

And can't help but wonder why?

Ok, so we know how this all started

(When the police killed Mark)

But that's no reason for riots and looting

And if you believe that you are living in the dark

We are ruled by a corrupt government

Guided by the secretive monarch

And whist we are living in the "depression"

They're spending stolen tax money on cars

Police being paid to murder

Politicians committing fraud

And as we struggle to stay afloat

Them fuckers are chilling abroad.

The people are frustrated and the tension suffocates

Murder sparked the riots. Now the fallen angels awake

It's almost like the people have been taken over, possessed
As the evil in their faces and their actions strongly suggest

They burn down many buildings

Smash everything in sight

With no care or thought for anyone

In the middle of the night

All the shops are looted

Faces are filled with delight

They carry more than they can manage

And these people know wrong from right

On every news channel you see them

From the BBC to CNN

Like a big fucking advertisement

Encouraging the yobs to do it again

So from one area to another

The malignity it spreads

And as we fear for our lives

Royals and government officials are tucked up nicely in bed

Some say that it's a conspiracy

The 'New World Order' in affect

The plan of the illuminati

To trick then dominate and oppress

I don't know if there is any truth in it

Right now anything is easy to believe

As I observe this corner of our world

As it weeps like a wound that bleeds.

Nothing Ever Stays the Same

With each and every second
Each circumstance will change
From situations certain
To tragic re-arrange
From a burning candle
To a disintegrated flame,
Once all the wax has melted
The wick wont light again.

A foetus nourished and protected
In her mother's womb
Surviving in amniotic fluid
Encased in her very own tomb.
In an instant she's cold and she's screaming
Eyes uncomfortably filling with light
As she is unwillingly delivered
In the middle of the night.

What used to be a loving family
Is broken, unhappy, estranged.
Parents tired of trying
When the problems remain the same.
Children getting caught up in the middle
Suffering broken and unsatisfied hearts
Hoping their parents will stay together
Whilst anticipating the next fight to start.

A conversation is cherished
When a loved one is here no more.
You keep going over the last time
You watched them walk out of the door
You're wishing you didn't take for granted
That you would see them again.
Regretting you didn't say "I love you"
Unknowing that that was the end.

Everything happens for reasons
Of which we are all puzzled and unsure.
Though we can all be certain
What was, there will be no more.
We sleep so we can wake,
We live until we die
Everything ALWAYS changes
and we will never understand why?

Baby Mother

When you're dealing with everything
And your man is elsewhere.
Baby girl I understand, trust me
I have been there!

When the baby needs changing,
Cupboards rearranging and mess is everywhere
You're thinking of him and wondering
"Why the hell ain't he here?!"

There's the kitchen to clean
And to load the machine
The shopping won't do itself
Hunny trust me,
I know what it's like to have to do it all by yourself!!

Surrounded in chaos, drowning in noise
So sick of picking up all these damn toys,
Sister you think he don't really care,
Coz if he did surely things would be fair!

When the house is quiet. Kids are fed
And you are so tired all you want is your bed
In he walks wit his hungry belly,
He kicks off his shoes and sits in front the telly.

No "How was your day?" or "Missed you today!"
Not one piece of appreciation coming your way
You look at the man you've been missing all day
You think, "If he was here would he help anyway?"

Baby Mother...
We both know the answer to this.
Look, he's fallen asleep.
Not even a kiss!

R.I.P Mark Duggan

People screaming

Buildings a blast

What the fuck??

How'd this all start??

Because the police murdered our brother Mark!!

This was the spark which ignited the flame

Which spread pandemonium across the U.K

Communities destroyed,

Homes burnt to the ground

Shops cleaned out and looted by everyone around.

Violence is spreading

War against the police

Who despite their authority are seemingly weak!

Vigilantes are out now and in full force

BNP with bats

Sikhs with holstered swords

People are living in fear now

The atmosphere is tense

The conflict of feelings is incredibly immense

I just want this to be over

For normality to be restored

So my children can carry on living and playing happily outdoors.

This poem is featured in the award winning documentary 'Riot From Wrong' - Produced and Directed By Teddy Nygh and the Fully Focused Team.

Free Your Minds

Why blame the white man for what you have not done?
Why highlight the fight and believe the battle was never won?
There is no denying the brutal facts,
The pain and suffering from lashings on backs.
In history, their stories etched in our minds.
The slave labour the teachers describe.
The picture history tells, makes us angry, hurt and hateful,
Well,
Instead of using it as an excuse not to create
from the abundance which is in our face.
Take the freedom they won for us and don't let it waste.
Stop killing each other, stop hating on your friends.
Put down your guns and pick up your pens!
You see the white man can't stop us from educating ourselves,
He can't stop us from generating wealth.
He can't stop us with whips and chains.
He can be the one though, that we all blame
As we don't evolve and are full of shame.
Yes they rule the land and made the law
But they don't close those open doors.
With ignorance we oppress ourselves.
We stay in the ghetto enslaved with no wealth.

Bob Marley was right when he spoke these few words.
From this little phrase there is a lot we can learn.

**"Emancipate YOURSELF from mental slavery,
none but ourselves can free our minds."**

This we should practise in no given time.

Educate yourselves and pass that to your young.
Don't teach them with scales or hand them down your guns.
Don't pass the opportunities you have to be great.
Use your god given talents without any haste.
Be leaders and stand up for what is right.
Hold your heads high with dignity and use your brains to fight!
Lead by example the greatness we possess.
Let go of the tarnishes of our race.
Make a world that we are proud to face
So we can leave behind the reputation of disgrace.
Build your empires, gain your wealth
Be proud to stand up and be yourself!
Face the fears as hard as they seem
And live for our ancestors what they only saw in dreams.
So When our children's children sit down for history lesson.
They will be inspired by love and count all their blessings.

Who's Sick?

Who are we to say they ain't right?

Because they don't view the world as you or I?

Because they don't give a damn about what they wear

They may not ever comb their hair

Because they may sometimes shout and swear

The truth is, maybe no one ever cared

Maybe, just maybe their childhood was bad

Maybe, it's possible, they were abused by their dad

Being dealt a hand of misery

could have meant they lost the game

And finally gave up and gave in to the pain.

Life after that would never be the same as "Mentally Ill" would

become their new name.

Who are we to say "They don't make any sense."

Because they now live a life of minimal stress

Because they have friends who reside in their heads?

Because they laugh at things we can't see,

Because they live a life that's free?

Maybe, just maybe they are very special,

In touch and blessed on a spiritual level,

It's possible they laugh coz we think they are mad,

When they know that it's the other way round.

Maybe, just maybe, we are the crazy ones?

Living in environments the government run

Paying for food which grows on trees...

Which I'm sure god intended to be free??

Sending our children to comprehensive schools

Allowing them to be taught by god knows who.

Going to work a 9-5, to pay your bills, what kinda life?

Walking around with miserable straight faces, missing all the

Amazing places,

Living in the gutter we make in our minds,

To the bigger picture we are blind....

If you ask me,

We are the mentally ill ones.

Consumer Consumption

Please allow me to introduce myself
I'm the greed, the pain, the hunger the wealth.
I'm the devil inside who is filled with pride consumed by ugly feelings and collapsing inside.

I'm the one who makes you forget those who are dear
I'm the one who acts so tough but is full of fear...
Loving the money the fame and all the status brings.
I'm that bastard inside who keeps pulling them strings...
Oh the clothes and the jewellery decorate my skin still I'm the insecurity that lies within.

The jealous rage when I don't get my own way.
The one who leaves because it's harder to stay.
Oh I can only commit to the grind on the streets.

BUT

I'll grind any girl between the sheets.
I'm that winner in everybody else's eyes.
But if I'm true to myself I'm losing inside.

"The Dark Side"

If I Go To Sleep

If I go to sleep and you cannot wake me
Please don't be sad for the lord has taken me
I am kept warm in a blanket of love
Which is made of the memories of all those I did love.

If my eyes are closed to never open again
Don't cry or be sad this is not the end
Remember my laugh, my smiles and good times
I'm in your thoughts so cannot die

If I should lie down and not get up
My time ran out, the clock was struck
It's ok. Don't feel no way
Just remember me and smile today

If I am motionless and blind, don't remember the bad times
Arguments and rows are meaningless now
Don't feel bad, please don't be low
Breathe deeply my friend and let it all go

If I go to sleep and you cannot wake me
Help me please by helping my babies
Comfort them when in the need
Educate them with our memories

I am asleep
I didn't die
You can see me
Just close your eyes

Grim Reaper

He wants to take me

And I don't know why

But every time I turn my back

He puts his scythe up high

And I don't know why

And I just want to cry

Because I love my life

And I don't want to die

They say the good die young

So I ponder being bad

Just so my life can go on

And I know that's wrong

But the fear is strong

My mind and body are tired

But I have to fight on!!

Flashbacks

I sit here crying

I'm getting flashbacks

Every time I relax

They seem to come back

I'm in recovery

I can't breathe

My mind is awake

But my body asleep

My lungs can't move

My legs are numb

They pull out the tube

I choke on my tongue

I've lived a nightmare

You know the ones

Where someone's trying to get you

But your feet won't run

But only this shit was REAL

It happened to me

And as it did I prayed to God "Please I don't want to leave!"

Cancer Filled Room

Sitting here on this decrepit chair

The sight of bald heads and thinning hair

The scent of worry, air full of fear

I wonder

What am I doing here?

The walls are drabby and ceiling is grey

No hope between these walls, spirits stolen away

As I await the doctor moaning I hear

And I think

I just don't fit in here!

It's like a place for the living dead

And just like the disease the sadness spreads

The vibe in this room is filled with doom

Can't wait to get out of this cancer filled room!

Haiku

I feel severe pain

Dark and excruciating

Almost unbearable

Tears

There are thousands of us here, in this dark, claustrophobic place.

We fight so hard to get out but we are held securely in place.

There are times when the yearning for freedom is incredibly hard to bear.

Trapped and cramped and in squashed conditions just dying to get out of here.

Fighting to be front of the queue as escaping is only a reality for a few.

Confusion and panic set in as we have no idea what to do.

Not wanting anything in particular, our purpose is unknown to us.

But the ambition to get out is so strong we use all our will not to combust!

We look for the white light which is situated at the end of the dark tunnel,

As soon as we glimpse the opening, we gel together and slide as though through a funnel.

Those of us at the front line break out as we only have seconds to flee,

Before the heavy exit slams closed leaving most of us trapped unnecessarily.

Once out we become individual, find freedom as we slide down her face.

We soak into the comfortable pillow finding our final resting place.

Silence

My silence is louder than the crashing of waves
More eerie than a ton of graves
And darker than the deepest caves.

My silence doesn't speak volumes
It screams them!
It creates a path for my unspoken words that soothes them.

It wasn't always silent
In fact, far from
Conversation once would roll off of my tongue.

Circumstances occurred
And slowly the silence crept in
Tired from repeating the same words over and over again

Trying to explain the feeling of pain whilst you are feeling it is not an easy task
So no longer do I explain myself, I simply wait until I'm asked.

I find comfort in my own mind which is a far from quiet place
But I completely understand ME
So in there I feel quite safe.

My silence has been triggered in so many different ways
Being hurt, lied to and more than once betrayed.

Having to justify your pain to the people who cause it
is a madness in itself
It's exhausting and frustrating and detrimental to the inner-self.

Re living trauma, reoccurring paranoia
Because you have lost trust
Trying to forgive, trying to forget
When you believe there has been an injustice.

I cry on the inside
I cry there every day
Even when I seem happy
I cry same way

I'm trying to figure out how to break it
I've tried with all of my might
But my phenomenal intuition is telling me, something isn't right.

I need to be kind, loving and supportive in every single way
And not just to everybody else, but throw some my own way.

I need to believe in myself
And in the power invested in me
To be able to master turning any situation into positive energy.

"I See The Light."

It's Not That Bad

I woke up this morning, wearing a frown
Feeling really sad and very down
Everything I want, I have and more
So this mournfulness makes me feel insecure.
Although I laugh, I smile, I play
Something inside me dies every day
There are things that I know, Things I can't share
No one I can TRUST to listen, though I know people care.
With an abundance of friends around me still,
This loneliness is hard to kill.
I try to shake it off, hold the dolefulness down
I think of u Grandad, Wish u were still around.

So I'm thinking..........

Well my life could be worse
A lady from the next block left town in a hearse
My sister, she can never have kids
My cousin don't know where her man is
The old boy upstairs don't know his own name
Three generations were wiped out in flames
There's a girl on the corner with a belt around her arm
Oblivious the shop she's just burgled is sounding alarm
A little boy on my road plays outside all alone
Whilst his daddy beats the hell out of mummy at home.

That's just the local commentary
What about worldwide devastation in just the last century??

China. 1931: between two to four million people gone
Washed away like shells on the shore
As the floods ran through for three months and more.
Dec 26 2004: An earthquake tore the Indian Ocean floor
Leaving around 230,000 dead, millions homeless, people unfed.
Billions and billions of people deceasedFrom famine,

hurricanes, landslides, disease
Since the 1970's Aids has killed an enormous 21.8 mill
And every year with no mistake 2 to 5 million Malaria takes.
Terrorist attacks on the London tube
Because of a lasting presidential feud
Wars in Iraq, Afghanistan, Iran
Many fallen soldiers, the innocent, their young

So now I'm thinking............................

Ok ... So My life is not the best, but in comparison I am blessed
It's really not as bad as it seems,
There will always be somebody that is worse off than me
The tough times, well they come with the great
They make me strong enough to deal with fate

Soldier

I see my life as a battle ground
Many wars and fights, ever victory bound
Sometimes knocked to the ground
Sometimes knocked for six
But I just get back up, using them survival tricks
My mind is powerful
And my soul is deep
Whatever the challenge, or how hard
I will soldier it and defeat!

From war wounds to battle scars
On my body is a mix
It's forever breaking down
And I'm forever trying to fix
But most importantly my mind is a powerful thing
And when the surgeons cut me open
My mind heals it from within
A fighting spirit
A soldier's soul
These two weapons used together beat any scalpel

Beat drug addictions
Left abusive homes
Shit I'm growing two children on my own
Cancer in my body, had a kidney taken out
Chemotherapy
Painkillers
Injecting myself

"Let the battle commence!" that's what I say
I believe I will beat whatever's thrown my way
And if I don't, I'll go out with pride
All guns blazing
With God by my side.

You Will Get By

There are times in your life things will go wrong

Where you can't force a smile or break into song

As the pain you feel turns you as hard as steel

In that sudden instant you realise shit just got real

Take a deep breath and simplify
With **God** by your side, you will get by!!

When your mind is plagued with worry and guilt

When not one person can break the barrier you've built

Storing secrets and telling lies, hiding from others in your own mind

Not seeing clearly almost completely blind

Take a deep breath and simplify
With **God** by your side you will get by!

When you feel so down and you cannot sleep

No one to talk too stress reaches its peak

These are the times that for **him** you must seek

For he carries your burdens, that was his sacrifice

So to **God** give thanks and live an abundant life

Take a deep breath and simplify
With **God** by your side, YOU WILL GET BY!!

"If you don't laugh, you cry."

Lamb Chop

I made a mistake...

A big one at that I gave something away I can never get back.

I dedicated my time.

I shared my space.

I comforted and advised.

I put him first place.

I listened to problems

I gave a shoulder to cry

I scrubbed cuffs and collars, hung shirts to dry.

I picked up after,

I followed behind.

I did all this stuff.. I didn't mind.

I'd listen to stories of his past girls.

Without even realising I was part of HIS world.

But something happened.

I knew it had to stop...

When he felt no way eating my last lamb chop!!!

I Ain't Giving Up My Seat

I am in the seat that you offer to people in the most need.
Wearing an oversized Nike tracksuit with a bulging knee..
There are people all around staring at me,
I stare right back and fix on an old lady.

Now she looks at me with daggers in her eyes
they say "give me that seat you selfish child"
I look at her and I smile anyway because I ain't giving up this seat lady.. not today!

So I turn my head and look the other way. My eyes fix on a man standing in a doorway, he has a broken leg and a walking stick he has his full body weight resting on it.
He looks at me and his eyes plead, but I don't care I still ain't giving up this seat.

Right in front of me stands a pregnant woman,
she's looking at me and she's rubbing her belly,
Now I must admit it looks rather heavy,
I know she's thinking "Get up already "
I look at her with a big huge smile. I'm thinking "Don't look for my seat I'll be here for a while."

Then all of a sudden someone speaks. They say. "Aren't you gonna offer someone your seat?" I look around and think "Are they talking to me? Nahh surely they really can't be."
I hear it again. "No manners in this day and age" and that little phrase sends me into a rage!

I stand up slowly and begin to talk, they move in closer thinking I'm gonna walk. I say "I know you all want this seat but believe no one needs it more than me! AND in fact I was brought up well because I'm doing what the sign says even though you can't tell.

You see that old lady may be old, and that man may have a stick and this lady is pregnant but I am sick!
I have Cancer, how looks do deceive? They not long took my right kidney that was major was surgery?
And this thing here bulging," I point at my knee.
"That's a bag that carries my wee.
So fuck if I'm offering any of you my seat,
At the moment I am I'm the most need!"

Now with all that said I look at the three and casually ask them all individually " Would you like this seat?"

I wait for a second and I listen carefully.
"Yeah as I thought this seat belongs to me."
I sit back down and can't help but smile as I watch them cringe and feel embarrassed for a while!

I Can't Stand Spoilt Kids

She's sleeping in the back pack
Looks so angelic and cute
But I bet you when she wakes up
She's a naughty likkle brute!
You know one of them spoilt ones
(usually they're white)
Their parent give them everything
But no discipline in sight.

Tantrums on the street
Flinging themselves down
The embarrassed parent whispers
"Darling calm down."
Calm down? I think....
Rahh what is this
I look at the mum thinking
"Love, are you taking the piss?"
I look at my kids and I calmly say
"You'd better not ever try that shit uh uh no way!"

Sometimes you see them
In the park
Clothes un-matching, left to do what they want
You see little girl children
With their matted heads
And the mums like
"She won't let me comb it so I just use clips instead!"
Won't let you?? Woman are you for real?
"You'd better sit your ass down
Unless you want to feel!"

These little spoilt brats
They really take the piss.
And when my kids see them
They wanna try that shit!
If your kid is 5 and he's calling you a bitch
Fuck the naughty step,
He needs some licks!!

Beware Of the Feeder

When you first met him you were looking hot,
Belly hanging over your jeans waist? I think not,
Looking so good you dazzled his mind
His brain started working overtime.

"Yo this girl gonna be mines, trust me on that.
Gonna have to feed her up though, make her fat!"

And you, you're smiling all up in his face
With no idea of the plan he's about to embrace
You're thinking "Aww he likes me for who I am!"
Whilst he gets underway with his master plan!

"Come babes, let's go out and eat,
Anything you want yea, don't worry my treat!"

So with all the wining and dining, chocolates all that
You're all loved up and slowly getting fat.
"I need to go gym." says the voice in your head
Then he whips out the chocolate body paint and says.

"Come babe, let's exercise in bed!"

Birthdays, Valentines and Christmas can't pass
Without boxes of chocolates and a full wine glass.
Those cosy nights in are long long gone
As you sit home alone wondering "Why ain't he home?"
It's 2AM when the phone starts to blow.

"Babe you want a Big Mac meal??, KFC's closed!"

And then one day, it suddenly clicks.
You look in the mirror and you think "Damn what is this??"
The clothes don't fit, the shirt's too tight
The button won't do up on the jeans without a fight,

He's looking at you and he's shaking his head.
"Bwoyyy babes, look how your belly's spread
And you know say the mattress is broke on your side of the bed!"
In bed all alone, disbelieving his words
You just cannot believe the way he turned up his nose.
You hear him then, voice muffled through the bedroom wall...
He's in the bathroom taking a call?

"I know, I'm sorry babe but I'm gonna be late
But don't worry I'm gonna make it up to you
I'm bringing custard and cake!!"

Printed in Great Britain
by Amazon.co.uk, Ltd.,
Marston Gate.